Askews 18·10·84

KU-605-805

The Book of Sweets

WITHDRAWN

The Book of Sweets

Patricia Lousada

EBURY PRESS

Published by Ebury Press
National Magazine House
72 Broadwick Street
London W1V 2BP

First impression 1984

© Patricia Lousada 1984
© Illustrations E T Archive Ltd 1984

Edited, designed and illustrated by
the E T Archive Ltd, Chelsea Wharf,
15 Lots Road, London SW10 0QH

Designer Julian Holland
Photography Eileen Tweedy

All rights reserved. No part of this publication
may be reproduced, stored in a retrieval system,
or transmitted, in any form or by any means,
electronic, mechanical, photocopying, recording
or otherwise, without prior permission of the
publishers.

ISBN 85223 373 6

Phototypeset in Great Britain by
Tradespools Limited, Frome, Somerset
Printed and bound by New Interlitho s.p.a., Milan

CUMBERNAULD & KILSYTH
DISTRICT LIBRARY

ACC. NO. 138952

CLASS NO.
641.85

VENDOR	DATE
Askews	18·10·8

Contents

Introduction

A pretty box filled with homemade sweets is a special treat for everyone. Fudge which was responsible for awakening many an initial interest in cooking, is only one of the delicious sweets which can be made at home. Popcorn balls, candied cranberries, turkish delight and sesame squares—to name but a few, are well within the range of any cook. Homemade sweets are fun to make and particularly satisfying when they look almost professional and often taste better than those professionally made! Scrumptious chocolate truffles are perhaps the easiest and the best of all. Even young children can help shape and roll the balls. Small fingers can also model marzipan fruits and nuts.

Many sweets such as nougat, humbugs and caramels are based on a boiled sugar syrup. These are not difficult to make but the recipes must be followed accurately because the degree to which the syrup is cooked determines the texture of the finished sweet.

Basic equipment for making sweets

A cool non-porous surface such as marble.

A large metal baking sheet can also be used.

A heavy, deep, good quality saucepan made from unlined copper, brass, stainless steel or aluminium. It must cook the syrup evenly and withstand the high temperatures required.

A good easy-to-read sugar thermometer.

A palette knife.

Rules for sugar syrups

Using a Thermometer

Keep the thermometer in a jar of hot water until the sugar has completely dissolved and then add it to the syrup. Make sure the bulb is well covered. Do not move it while it is in the syrup. Read it at eye-level. When the required temperature is reached place it back in the jar of hot water. Wash and dry separately and store in a safe place.

Making the Sugar Syrup

Place the required amounts of cold water and sugar into a heavy saucepan. Stir the syrup gently, over a medium heat, so that it does not splash on to the sides of the pan and crystallise. Remove any drops by brushing them away with a pastry brush dipped in hot water. Once the syrup is clear bring it to the boil and continue boiling without stirring until the desired temperature is reached.

Crystallisation

Sugar has a natural tendency to revert back to its crystallised form. Even a few grains left in a syrup can start the process.

Liquid glucose, lemon juice and cream of tartar are included in recipes because they act as interfering agents and help avoid crystallisation of the syrup. Liquid glucose is the most effective and is essential for some boiled sweets. Fats and milk solids also impede crystallisation and must be stirred occasionally to prevent burning.

Crystallisation is desirable in some sweets. Beating a syrup while it is hot promotes the natural tendency of the sugar to grain. The hotter the syrup when it is beaten, the grainier the consistency. Fudge is left to cool slightly before it is beaten to achieve a fine grain.

Chocolate

Professionals use a special chocolate called *couverture* for coating purposes. It is hard to obtain and must be tempered before it can be used. This involves heating it to 105–110°C/200–205°F. Cooling it to about 75°C/145°F and reheating it to 90–95°C/175–180°F for coating.

Satisfactory results can be achieved by using good plain eating chocolate and adding a small amount of oil. Complete directions are given on page 28.

Do not be tempted to use the inexpensive chocolate covering that is easily available. It has a poor flavour and can ruin the sweets.

Measures

1 teaspoon (tsp) = 5 ml
1 tablespoon (tbsp) = 15 ml

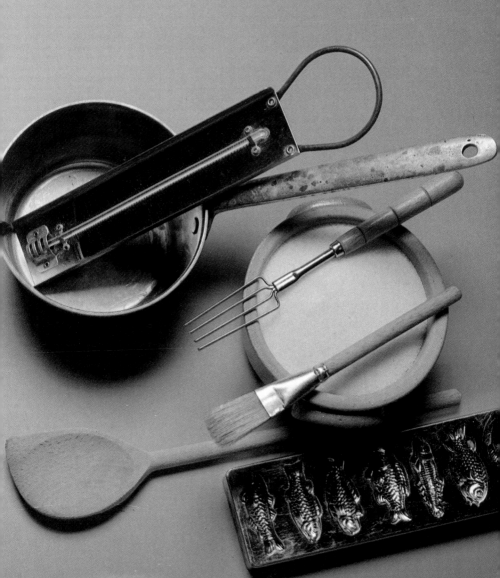

Peppermint Humbugs and Fruit-Flavoured Sweets

For the humbugs
250 g (8 oz) demerara sugar
75 ml (3 fl oz) water
15 g (½ oz) butter
1 tbsp black treacle
pinch of cream of tartar
4–5 drops oil of peppermint

For the fruit-flavoured sweets
250 g (8 oz) granulated sugar
75 ml (3 fl oz) water
6 tbsp lemon juice
1 tbsp liquid glucose
a few drops of colouring.
flavouring, 1 tsp may be enough

For the humbugs: oil a marble slab, or work surface, a palette knife, and a pair of rubber gloves. Place all ingredients, except the peppermint, in a heavy saucepan. Stir over a moderate heat to dissolve the sugar. Brush down the side of the pan frequently with a pastry brush dipped in water. Boil, with only an occasional stir, until the syrup reaches 140°C/285°F. Remove from the heat, and add the oil of peppermint. Pour the mixture on to the prepared surface, and, with the palette knife, fold it towards the centre as it spreads out. Wearing rubber gloves, and working as quickly as possible, pull off a third of the candy, and set aside. Pull and twist the larger piece into a long sausage shape. Fold and pull it until it becomes opaque. Meanwhile, give the smaller piece a little pull to prevent it from hardening. When the larger piece is an opaque rope, add the darker piece pulled to a similar length. Twist them together to make a rope of alternating colour. Cut into pieces, giving the rope a half turn towards you with each cut, to shape into cushions.

For the fruit-flavoured sweets: oil a marble slab, or work surface, a palette knife, and a pair of rubber gloves. Place the sugar, glucose and water in a heavy saucepan, and bring to a temperature of 116°C/240°F. Add the lemon juice and colouring, and boil the syrup to a temperature of 149°C/300°F. Take off the heat, add the flavouring and pour on to the prepared work surface. Follow the humbug recipe for the turning, pulling and cutting of the sweets.

For the lollipops on title page:
Follow the recipe for fruit-flavoured sweets. Allow syrup to reach 143°C/290°F. Add flavouring and spoon small circles of the syrup onto an oiled surface. Press a stick into each circle, then spoon a few drops of syrup over each stick. Leave to set before wrapping individually in cellophane.

Rocky Road

To make about 600 g (1¼ lb)

12 marshmallows
75 g (3 oz) walnuts, pecans or almonds or a
  mixture of any
450 g (1 lb) milk chocolate

Dice the marshmallows and roughly chop the nuts. Line a baking tray with non-stick parchment paper. Break the chocolate into small pieces and place them in the top of a double saucepan set over hot but not boiling water. Stir until the chocolate melts then add the marshmallows and nuts, and pour onto the prepared tin. With an oiled palette knife smooth over the surface covering any nuts and marshmallows with the chocolate. Leave to set before breaking into pieces.

A variation using banana

450 g (1 lb) milk chocolate
100 g (4 oz) dried banana chips

Line a baking sheet with non-stick baking parchment. Melt the chocolate as in the above recipe. When the chocolate has melted, add the banana chips and pour onto the prepared tin. Spread with an oiled palette knife and leave to set before breaking into pieces.

Any dried fruit or combination of fruits or nuts can be used in place of banana.

Popcorn Balls and Caramel Coated Popcorn

For the balls
1 tbsp oil
75 g (3 oz) popping corn
200 g (7 oz) granulated sugar
2 tbsp liquid glucose
50 ml (2 fl oz) water
1 tbsp vanilla extract
butter for greasing

For the caramel coated popcorn
1 tbsp oil
75 g (3 oz) popping corn
25 g (1 oz) butter
250 g (9 oz) soft dark brown sugar
6 tbsp water

For the balls: to pop the corn; place the oil and popping corn in a large, heavy saucepan and set over medium heat. Cover the pan and shake or swirl it over the heat until you begin to hear the corn popping (5–10 minutes). Keep shaking the pan until there are no more pops. Pour the popcorn into a greased bowl and place in a warm oven 130°C/250°F/mark ½ while making the syrup. Stir the sugar, glucose and water in a small heavy-bottomed saucepan over moderate heat until the sugar is dissolved. Brush down the sides of the pan frequently with a pastry brush dipped in water. Bring to a boil and boil without stirring until the

temperature reaches 132°C/270°F. Remove from the heat and add the vanilla extract and the warmed popcorn. Mix together with a wooden spoon and then as soon as the mixture can be handled without burning, quickly form into tennis-size balls with buttered hands. Place them on greaseproof paper to cool before wrapping individually in cellophane or cling film.

For the caramel coated popcorn: pop the corn following the above instructions. Stir the butter, brown sugar and water over moderate heat until the sugar dissolves. Boil without stirring until the temperature reaches 112°C/234°F. Stir the syrup into the popcorn until every kernel is coated.

Sesame Crunch

To make about 450 g (1 lb)

225 g (8 oz) granulated sugar
100 g (4 oz) butter
175 g (6 oz) sesame seeds
squeeze of lemon

Line an 18 cm (7 inch) square tin with non-stick baking parchment. Place the sugar and butter in a small heavy saucepan and stir over moderate heat until the sugar is dissolved. Add the sesame seeds and continue to cook, stirring occasionally until the mixture turns a good caramel colour. Take off the heat, add the lemon juice and pour into the prepared tin. Before it sets, score the top into squares or rectangles. When it is cold, cut or break along the score lines. Wrap individually and store in an airtight container.

Vanilla and Chocolate Caramels

To make about 450 g (1 lb) of each

For the vanilla caramels
275 g (10 oz) granulated sugar (preferably
  vanilla sugar)
275 g (10 oz) double cream
2 tbsp liquid glucose
1 vanilla pod, split lengthwise
1 tsp vanilla extract

For the chocolate caramels
all ingredients as for vanilla
caramels plus—
75 g (3 oz) plain chocolate
25 g (1 oz) cocoa powder

Grease and line a 20 cm (8 inch) square baking tin with non-stick baking parchment. Stir the sugar, cream, liquid glucose and vanilla pod in a heavy saucepan over moderate heat until the sugar is dissolved. Brush down the sides of the pan frequently with a pastry brush dipped in water. Bring to a boil, and boil with only an occasional stir until the syrup reaches 121°C/250°F on a sugar thermometer. Remove the pan from the heat and set the base in cold water to stop further cooking. Remove the vanilla pod and add the vanilla essence, Quickly pour the syrup into the tin and leave to set. Unmould and cut into squares and wrap the pieces in cellophane.

For the chocolate caramels: follow the recipe for the vanilla caramels. When removing the vanilla pod add chocolate and cocoa with the vanilla extract. Stir to blend then quickly pour into the prepared tin. Cut into squares when set, and wrap the pieces in cellophane.

Buttons and Lace

To make about 450 g (1 lb)

450 g (1 lb) plain chocolate in small pieces
2 tbsp sunflower or groundnut oil
hundreds and thousands
wine or beer thermometer

Boil a small amount of water in the bottom of a double saucepan. The bottom of the top pan should not touch the water and should fit tightly to avoid steam coming in contact with the chocolate. Take the pan off the heat and add the chocolate and oil. Cover the pan and leave for several minutes, stirring occasionally, until the pieces have melted. The chocolate should not exceed a temperature of 55°C/110°F. Allow the chocolate to drop to a temperature of 45°C/90–95°F before using for buttons, lace or coating. Line 2 baking sheets with non-stick parchment paper. To make the buttons; drop the chocolate from a teaspoon onto the paper to form rounds or pipe rounds through an icing bag. Sprinkle with hundreds and thousands while still wet. To make the lace: using an icing bag fitted with a number 2 nozzle, pipe into lace-like patterns. Allow the chocolate to become hard before peeling it away from the paper and packaging.

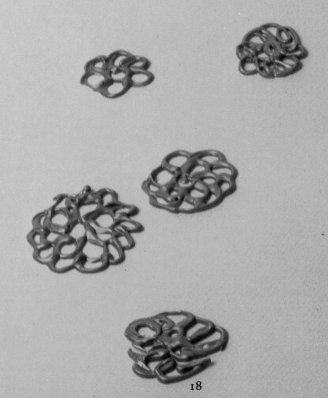

Stuffed Prunes and Dates

To make about 450 g (1 lb)

225 g (8 oz) dates
225 g (8 oz) ready-to-eat pitted prunes
100 g (4 oz) ground almonds
50 g (2 oz) caster sugar
2–3 tbsp lemon juice, rosewater (not triple
  strength), white rum, bourbon or 1 tbsp
  vanilla extract
25 g (1 oz) shelled pistachio nuts, finely
  chopped

Cut a slit in each date and remove the stone.
Mix the ground almonds and caster sugar
together. Stir in the flavouring you are
using and enough water to make a paste.
Form into small balls and fill the cavity left
by the stone or pit. Roll in the pistachio
nuts and pack in individual sweet papers.

Prunes stuffed with chocolate
To make about 900 g (2 lb)

250 g (9 oz) plain chocolate, in small pieces
225 ml (8 fl oz) double cream
50 g (2 oz) unsalted butter
2 tbsp Armagnac or brandy
50 g (2 oz) walnuts, chopped
900 g (2 lb) ready-to-eat pitted prunes
caster sugar

Place the chocolate, cream and butter in the
top of a double saucepan over barely simmering water. Stir the mixture until the
chocolate melts. Take off the heat, cool and
refrigerate for several hours until firm.
Work in the Armagnac and walnuts. Pull
off small pieces of the chocolate, form into
balls and fill the prunes. Roll in caster sugar
and package in one layer, in a shallow box,
covered with cling film or foil. Refrigerate
until ready to use.

New Orleans Pralines

To make about 600 g (1¼ lb)

350 g (12 oz) soft dark brown sugar
50 g (2 oz) butter
4 tbsp water
175 g (6 oz) pecan nuts
1 tsp vanilla extract

Butter two baking sheets. Place the sugar,
butter and water in a small heavy-bottomed
saucepan and stir over moderate heat until
the sugar dissolves. Add the pecan nuts and
cook, stirring, until it reaches a temperature of 115°C/238°F on a sugar thermometer. Remove the pan from the heat
and add the vanilla extract; leave to cool for
2 minutes. Stir for a few seconds and drop it
on the baking sheets in spoonfuls about
5 cm (2 in) in diameter.

Caramelised Grapes and Orange Sections

2 navel oranges, peeled and divided into
  segments
12 large white grapes with stalks
450 g (1 lb) granulated sugar
few drops of lemon juice

Place the fruit on a tray and set over a
radiator for a few hours. Line a baking sheet
with parchment paper. Have a large saucepan at hand filled with enough boiling
water to come half-way up the sides of the
small heavy pan which will be used for
cooking the syrup. Melt the sugar in the
small pan over moderate heat, stirring
continuously with a wooden spoon. When
the sugar is completely melted and is a pale
golden colour remove from the heat and
place in the pan containing the boiled
water. Add the lemon juice and quickly dip
half a segment of orange and place on tray.
Continue dipping the remaining half segments and when they are cool enough to
handle dip the other halves. Dip the grapes
by holding the stems. Work quickly and if
the syrup does begin to harden reheat over
gently simmering water.

Nougat

To make about 750 g (1½ lb)

100 g (4 oz) skinned chopped hazelnuts
100 g (4 oz) blanched chopped almonds
75 g (3 oz) pistachio nuts
225 g (8 oz) granulated sugar
2 tbsp of liquid glucose
110 ml (4 fl oz) water
150 ml (5 fl oz) thin honey
2 egg whites, size 2
1 tsp vanilla extract

Oil and line a 25 × 20 × 6 cm (10 × 8 × 2½ in) tin with parchment paper covered with a sheet of rice paper. Cut another set of papers for the top. Lightly toast the nuts in a preheated oven 180°C/350°F/mark 4, for about 8 minutes. Warm the honey in a small saucepan over very gentle heat. Stir the sugar, glucose and water in a heavy pan over moderate heat until the sugar is dissolved. Brush down the sides of the pan frequently with a pastry brush dipped in water. When all the sugar grains have dissolved bring to the boil and boil over high heat without stirring until the temperature on a sugar thermometer reaches 138°C/280°F. Pour in the warmed honey and continue to boil until the syrup reaches 154°C/310°F. Meanwhile, whisk the egg whites in a large bowl over a pan of barely simmering water until they form stiff peaks. When the syrup reaches the correct temperature, pour it in a slow steady stream over the egg whites while continuing to whisk. Whisk, over simmering water, until the mixture thickens and begins to set. This can take several minutes and is more easily done with an electric hand beater. When the mixture is very stiff, fold in the nuts and flavouring and spoon into the prepared tin. The mixture's stiffness will make this quite hard to do. Use an oiled palette knife to push level, cover with the rice paper and then the parchment paper. Place a board over the mixture weighted with a heavy weight or a brick. Leave overnight to set before removing from the tin and cutting into bars. Wrap individually in cellophane or store in an airtight tin interleaved with parchment paper.

Prune Bonbons

To make 900 g (2 lb)

225 g (8 oz) soft prunes
100 ml (4 fl oz) Armagnac
250 g (9 oz) plain chocolate in small pieces
225 ml (8 fl oz) double cream
50 g (2 oz) unsalted butter
a few walnut pieces for decoration

For the coating

425 g (15 oz) plain chocolate in small pieces
2 tbsp sunflower or groundnut oil

Soak the prunes in the Armagnac and leave, covered, for at least five days. Place the chocolate, cream and butter in the top of a double saucepan, and, over barely simmering water, stir the mixture until the chocolate melts. Take off the heat and allow to cool. Strain the prunes, reserving any liquid. Remove the stones from the prunes, and cut them into pea-sized pieces. Stir the prunes into the ganache (chocolate mixture), and add 2 tbsp of the soaking liquid.

Seal the ganache with a layer of cling film pressed on to its surface, and refrigerate for 24 hours.

Line a baking sheet with non-stick parchment paper. Spoon out teaspoons of the ganache, and lightly form into balls by rolling between the palms. Place on the prepared sheet, and refrigerate for 1 hour, or up to 24 hours, before coating.

Coating the bonbons: Boil a small amount of water in the bottom of a double saucepan. The bottom of the top pan should not touch the water, and should fit tightly to avoid steam coming in contact with the chocolate. Take the pan off the heat, and add the chocolate and oil. Cover and leave until the chocolate has melted. The chocolate should not exceed a temperature of 43°C/110°F. Allow the chocolate to drop to a temperature of 40°–42°C/90°–95°F before coating.

Work with a few chocolates at a time, and keep the remainder refrigerated. Drop a chocolate into the coating, and turn with a fork to coat all over. Lift it out with the fork, and scrape the bottom of the fork against the edge of the pan to remove any excess chocolate. Slide the chocolate on to a baking sheet lined with non-stick baking parchment. Place a small piece of walnut on top of each chocolate before it sets. Eat within 9–10 days.

Muesli and Coconut Muesli Bars

To make about 450 g (1 lb)

75 g (3 oz) brown sugar
50 g (2 oz) butter
2 tbsp honey
2 tbsp water
1 tbsp oil
1 tsp vanilla extract
275 g (10 oz) muesli base which uses cereal flakes, raisins and nuts

Preheat the oven to 150°C/300°F/mark 2. In a saucepan, combine all the ingredients except the muesli base. Stir over low heat until the sugar dissolves. Pour over the muesli and mix well. Grease and line a 19 × 28 × 3.5 cm (8 × 12 × 1½ in) baking tin with non-stick baking parchment. Press the mixture over the base of the tin in an even layer. Bake for 20–25 minutes or until the muesli turns a pale golden colour. Score into bars while still warm. Leave in the tin to cool, cut the bars and wrap individually in cling film. Store in an airtight container.

Coconut muesli bars
To make about 450 g (1 lb)

100 ml (4 fl oz) sunflower oil
100 g (4 oz) unrefined sugar
2 tbsp honey
2 tsp vanilla extract
200 g (8 oz) cereal flakes
25 g (1 oz) sesame seeds
25 g (1 oz) desiccated coconut

Preheat the oven to 180°C/350°F/mark 4. Heat the oil, sugar and honey together over a low heat until the sugar dissolves. Remove from the heat and stir in the vanilla extract. Pour over the cereal flakes and mix well. Stir in the sesame seeds and coconut. Grease and line a tin approximately 33 by 24 cm (13½ by 9½ in) with non-stick baking parchment. Press the mixture over the base of the tin in an even layer. Bake for 25 minutes or until the flakes turn a golden brown. Score into bars while still warm. Leave in the tin to cool, cut the bars and wrap individually in cling film. Store in an airtight container.

Peppermint Creams

Makes about 500 g (1 lb)

350 g (12 oz) sugar
110 ml (4 fl oz) water
1 tsp lemon juice
a few drops of oil of peppermint
green colouring (optional)

Place sugar, water and lemon juice in a heavy saucepan. Stir carefully over a moderate heat to dissolve sugar. Brush down the sides of the pan with a pastry brush dipped in water. Boil without stirring until the syrup reaches a temperature of 116°C/ 240°F. Add the peppermint oil and colouring and pour on to a damp marble or other work surface. Allow to cool for several minutes before working with a damp spatula in a figure-of-eight motion. Scrape the edges toward the centre from time to time. Work for approximately 10 minutes, until the mixture becomes opaque and stiffens slightly. If the mixture is still quite soft, leave for 30 minutes. Form rounds by placing teaspoons of the fondant on a piece of non-stick baking parchment. If the fondant is too firm, warm it over a gentle heat to soften. Leave overnight at room temperature to become firm.

Turkish Delight

To make about 675 g (1½ lb)

600 ml (1 pint) water
25 g (1 oz) powdered gelatine
50 g (2 oz) cornflour
2 tbsp liquid glucose
575 g (1¼ lb) granulated sugar
grated rind of 1 orange
juice of 2 oranges and 1 lemon
50 g (2 oz) pistachio nuts, chopped
2 tbsp rose water, triple strength
4 drops red food colouring
cornflour
citric acid
icing sugar

Soften the gelatine in a bowl with 150 ml
(¼ pint) cold water. Slake the cornflower
with 150 ml (¼ pint) water in another bowl.
Dissolve the sugar and glucose with the
remaining 300 ml (½ pint) of water over a
medium heat. Bring to the boil and boil for
3 minutes. Add the cornflower, gelatine
and rind and boil stirring for a few minutes.
Add the orange and lemon juice, bring back
to the boil and boil for about 8 minutes
stirring occasionally. Take off the heat and
add the nuts, rose water and colouring. Line
a 22 cm (9 in) square tin with non-stick
parchment paper. Pour in the mixture and
when it begins to thicken but before it sets,
stir to distribute the nuts. Leave to become
firm, turn out and cut into squares. Toss in
cornflower and leave for a few hours. Toss in
icing sugar mixed with citric acid (a pinch
of citric acid to 25 g (1 oz) of sugar.) Leave
overnight before packing in a box with
plenty of mixed sugar and citric acid.

Maple Walnut and Chocolate Fudge

To make about 600 g (1¼ lb) of each

For the maple walnut fudge
175 ml (6 fl oz) pure maple syrup
225 ml (8 fl oz) milk
1 tbsp liquid glucose
25 g (1 oz) unsalted butter
75 g (3 oz) walnuts, chopped
1 tsp vanilla extract

For the chocolate fudge
400 g (14 oz) granulated sugar
225 ml (8 fl oz) milk
1 tbsp liquid glucose
75 g (3 oz) unsalted butter
50 g (2 oz) plain chocolate
40 g (1½ oz) cocoa powder
1 tsp vanilla extract
50 g (2 oz) walnuts, chopped

For the maple walnut fudge: oil a 20 × 20 cm (8 × 8 in) shallow cake tin and line the bottom with non-stick parchment paper. Combine the maple syrup, milk, sugar and glucose in a heavy-bottomed saucepan. Cook over moderate heat, stirring, until the sugar is dissolved. Cook without stirring (unless it threatens to stick) until the temperature reaches 114°C/238°F. Carefully remove the pan from the heat, add the butter but do not stir it in, and set the bottom of the pan in cold water. When the mixture cools to 43°C/110°F add the vanilla extract and walnuts and stir together to blend. Pour the mixture into the prepared tin and cut into squares when it is cool and set.

For the chocolate fudge: prepare tin as above. Combine the sugar, milk and glucose in a heavy saucepan and stir over moderate heat until the sugar dissolves. Cook without stirring until the temperature reaches 114°C/238°F; remove from the heat. Melt the chocolate and cocoa with the butter and pour into the syrup. Stir in the nuts and vanilla extract and pour into the tin. Cut into squares when set.

Candied Kumquats or Cranberries

450 g (1 lb) kumquats or cranberries or a
  mixture of both
300 ml (½ pint) water
350 g (12 oz) granulated sugar
caster sugar for coating

Kumquats need a slight poaching before they begin the candying process; this is not necessary for cranberries.

Gently heat the kumquats and water to just below a simmer. Drain the fruit, reserving the cooking liquid, and place the fruit in a shallow non-metallic dish. Add the uncooked cranberries to the same dish. Stir 175 g (6 oz) of sugar and the cooking liquid (or water if you are only doing cranberries) over moderate heat until the sugar dissolves. Brush down the sides of the

pan frequently with a pastry brush dipped in water. Bring to a good rolling boil, take off the heat and pour over the fruit. Press a sheet of greaseproof paper on the surface of the fruit, to help keep them submerged and leave for 24 hours.

The next day drain the syrup back into the pan, add 50 g (2 oz) of sugar and bring the syrup to the boil. Pour over the fruit, cover with the cartouche, and leave again for 24 hours. Repeat this process for 2 more days. Drain the fruit, keep the syrup in a closed jar in the refrigerator for another use such as fruit salads or sorbets. Roll the fruit in a shallow dish covered in caster sugar. Place the sugared fruit on a rack and leave to dry before packaging. The fruit should be eaten within a few days.

Chocolate Peanut Butter Toffees

To make about 800 g (1¾ lb)

450 g (1 lb) granulated sugar
50 g (2 oz) unsalted butter
squeeze of lemon
100 g (4 oz) smooth peanut butter

For the coating
450 g (1 lb) plain chocolate, in small pieces
2 tbsp sunflower or groundnut oil

Oil a non-porous work surface, a baking sheet, a palette knife, a rolling pin and a pair of rubber gloves. Preheat the oven to 150°C/300°F/mark 2.

Dissolve the sugar in a heavy saucepan over moderate heat stirring constantly with a wooden spoon. When the sugar has melted and is a pale golden colour add the butter and stir until melted. Remove from the heat, add a squeeze of lemon and pour on to the prepared surface. Wearing rubber gloves and using the palette knife, fold the mixture towards the centre as it spreads out and shape into a rectangle. Working as quickly as possible, spread the peanut butter over two-thirds of the caramel. Fold the plain one-third over the centre and the remaining one-third over the top—as for flaky pastry or a letter. Rotate the package 90 degrees, roll into a rectangle and repeat the folding sequence. If it is too hard to roll or fold, place on the baking sheet and put into the oven until pliable again. The peanut butter will ooze and look messy but with another few turns, folds and rolls it will amalgamate. It may have to be warmed between turns but when it has amalgamated roll it about 1.5 cm (½ in) thick and cut into squares. Cool before dipping in chocolate following the instructions for coating on page 28.

Marzipan Fruits and Nuts

Makes about 700 g (1½ lb)

For the marzipan
450 g (1 lb) granulated sugar
175 ml (6 fl oz) water
350 g (12 oz) ground almonds
1 tbsp liquid glucose
2 egg whites, lightly beaten
icing sugar
green, red, and orange food colouring
coffee essence for brown

For the icing dots
1 tbsp egg white
icing sugar

In a heavy saucepan stir the granulated sugar, water and glucose over moderate heat until sugar is dissolved. Boil without stirring until syrup reaches a temperature of 114°C/238°F. Off the heat stir in the ground almonds. Add the egg whites and return to a very low heat. Cook for only a minute or two, until the mixture becomes slightly firm.

Colour while the marzipan is still warm.
Chestnuts (green and brown): roll green into balls and brown into almonds. Make a dent in one side of the ball and insert almond. Shape into a chestnut.

Acorns (brown and green): Make a brown oblong and cover one end with a green tip.

Strawberries (red): roll into a ball then work one end to make a strawberry shape. Use a piece of angelica for the stalk.

Apples (green): form into balls. Blush with diluted red colouring. Use a clove for the calyx and a piece of vanilla pod for the stalk.

Oranges (orange): form into balls. Roll against a fine grater. Use cloves for stalk and calyx.

Pipe tiny dots on the chestnuts, acorns and strawberries using an icing made with icing sugar and egg white.

Chocolate Truffles

To make about 675 g (1½ lb)

For the ganache (chocolate paste)
200 ml (7 fl oz) single cream
25 g (1 oz) butter
1 vanilla pod
450 g (1 lb) plain chocolate in small pieces
2 tbsp rum, brandy or liqueur
25 g (1 oz) coarsely ground praline

For the coverings
4 tbsp cocoa
1 tbsp icing sugar
chocolate vermicelli

For the praline
100 g (4 oz) granulated sugar
100 g (4 oz) blanched hazelnuts

Heat the cream, butter and vanilla pod until it reaches a rolling boil. Remove from the heat and stir in the chocolate. When it has melted add the rum or brandy. Pour into a shallow tin lined with non-stick baking parchment and spread out. Leave in cool place uncovered for 24 hours. Pull off small pieces of chocolate and roll into balls. Incorporate the praline into some of them. Mix the cocoa with the icing sugar and roll truffles either in this or the vermicelli or the praline. Place in individual sweet papers and refrigerate until use.

To make the praline: place the nuts and sugar in a heavy small pan over moderate heat. Stir continuously until the sugar has melted and is a caramel colour. Pour onto an oiled tin or marble surface and let it harden. Break into pieces and pulverise with a rolling pin or in a blender or processor.

Almond Brittle

To make about 450 g (*1 lb*)

275 g (10 oz) granulated sugar
4 tbsp golden syrup
1 tbsp lemon juice
55 ml (2 fl oz) water
pinch of cream of tartar
225 g (8 oz) almonds

Oil a marble or non-porous flat surface or the back of a large baking tin. Combine the sugar, syrup, lemon juice, water and cream of tartar in a heavy-bottomed saucepan. Cook over moderate heat, stirring, until the sugar is dissolved. Brush down sides of the pan frequently with a pastry brush dipped in water. When all the sugar grains have dissolved, add the nuts and continue to stir until the syrup takes on a light caramel colour. Pour the mixture onto the prepared surface and spread as thinly as possible with an oiled spatula. Leave to cool before removing and breaking into pieces. Store in an airtight container.

Sweetheart

Why not put the sweets you have made from these recipes in one of the many different moulds available for shaping chocolate?

Polish the inside of the mould with a soft dry cloth so that the surface of the chocolate will be glossy. Spoon the melted chocolate into the mould and rotate the mould so the melted chocolate runs around the inside, completely coating the mould. Tip out the excess chocolate and leave inverted on a sheet of greaseproof paper until firm. Repeat the process to form a second layer. When the chocolate sets hard after several hours, it will shrink away from the mould and can be easily removed.